Writing Kibera

A literary work benefitting New Life Restoration Ministries serving the
children and families of the Kibera slum - Nairobi, Kenya

by The Kibera Writers

ISBN-13: 978-1495977152

ISBN-10: 1495977153

Special thanks to the editorial board:

Margaret Siegrist
Jay Siegrist
Marilyn Denney Blankenship

They helped this vision become alive - *Terry*

(Front cover art contributed by Jay and Margaret Siegrist)

Forward
by Jay Siegrist

I first met Paul and Grace Mbithi in 2009 while traveling to Kenya with a mission team led by Gail Castle of Leadership in Missions (LEAMIS). Also on the team were my wife (Margaret), my daughter (Megan), and my eldest son (Taylor) among others. Margaret and Megan had been on a previous trip there and had nothing but good things to say about Paul and Grace and the work they were doing with New Life Restoration Ministries. Megan had in fact stayed in Nairobi for a period of time after her first mission trip in order to work in an AIDS clinic. Paul and Grace took her into their home and provided her with support, protection, guidance, and most importantly love. Their children Ben and Julie were equally accepting and gracious even to the point of Julie offering to sleep on the floor so Megan could have her bed.

When I saw in person, what Paul and Grace were doing in the Kibera slums, how they tried to maximize the impact of their meager resources and the personal sacrifice required, I was truly blow away. The results could easily be read in the happy faces of the children at the school and orphanage. I was seeing springs of joy and hope coming forth in a desert of hopelessness. It was a very humbling experience to hear how they both gave up well paying careers (he was the freight manager for East Africa with KLM Airlines and she was with the Meteorology Department at the Nairobi Airport) in order to heed the call that God put in their hearts.

I am personally grateful to Terry Blankenship who wanted to help the children in Kibera by compiling this book as well as everyone who has contributed their time and effort. I can assure them as well as anyone who purchases this book, that any benefits that New Life Restoration Ministries receives will be spent wisely and any prayers on their behalf will not be wasted. I thank you all.

What this book is all about
by Terry Blankenship

I once had a friend far wiser than me tell me that if I wanted to catch fish, I had to get on the lake.

I wanted a way to raise some money for New Life Restoration Ministries (NLRM) to help the children of Kibera in one of Africa's largest slums and didn't know how to do it.

I had to figure it out. I had to get on the lake, so to speak.

So I had an idea of reaching out to my friends who were writers and putting out a small booklet of their writings on the theme of 'helping others', selling the book through whatever means I had at my disposal then turning all the proceeds over to NLRM.

I discussed this idea with my wife Marilyn and Jay and Margaret Siegrist, who all encouraged me to proceed. Pastor Paul Mbithi who leads NLRM was also very encouraging.

That is what this book is all about.

In addition to the writings of my friends and family, inside is the writing of a daughter of Paul and Grace Mbithi … writings of workers in the ministry in Kibera, and writings of students at Paul and Grace's school. We all have different gifts to contribute to the kingdom of God therefore the writers contained herein are contributing their gifts of words and creativity, in the hope of bringing gain to NLRM.
The main theme of 'helping others' is all through this book however any other theme was welcomed also. Therefore, you'll find poetry on nature and God, essays on life, writings on God and other topics contained herein. All writings have been offered as a gift to God.

I hope you enjoy it. Most of all, I hope you receive a blessing of joy in the knowledge that you have contributed to this worthwhile ministry.

New Life Restoration Ministries
(from NLRB website)

New Life Restoration Ministries is a faith-based organization. It was initiated with a vision of changing communities living in Kibera Slums, and other marginalized regions in Kenya   through spiritual nourishment, and socio-economic development as guided by the Gospel teaching, Luke 19:10 (reaching out to the Nations).

New Life Restoration Ministries, as a local church, has the burden of ensuring the well being of human beings as dignified by God himself both in the Old and New Testament.

The church is very close to the community members in Kibera slums where it is based. The founder members had the burden and vision of initiating the ministry to cater for the livelihood of its community through education support programs, micro-finance initiatives and environmental conservation activities, apart from the main holistic activities.

Kibera slums are some of the biggest slums in Africa. It is the second largest in Africa, after Soweto in South Africa. The population of the slum is composed of different communities with multi-cultural aspects. The total population is approximate to 900,000. The communities living in these slums are poor and very vulnerable to HIV/AIDS infections and transmission. Poverty has greatly contributed to very low living standards of the people. Majority are a product of intense rural urban migration in search of jobs and other social amenities. Illiteracy, drug abuse, commercial sex and child abuse are very common trends at the slums.

The congestion of the household results in overcrowding, thus creating rooms for other social evils. Children and the youth have become street children, commercial sex workers, drugs peddlers thereby wasting their potential and dignity of life as God given.

New Life Restoration Ministries initiated Springs of Life Children's Centre to offer care and psychosocial support to orphans and other

7

vulnerable children especially orphans due to HIV/AIDS, street children and other children in need of special protection.

The ministry set up micro finance project for women and the youth Income Generating Activities. The project for women is working towards empowering women for sustainable economic growth through utilizing local raw material to produce cottage products such as candles, soap and other commodities.

Poverty level is high in the slums due to lack of jobs and high population. The situation is worsened by presence of HIV/AIDS. This has facilitated many children to becoming orphans, and, ultimately, street children.

Currently the church ministry has grown into 60 branches in the East Africa Region in Kenya, Uganda and Tanzania.

The church is caring for hundreds of children through educational support via the establishment of Restoration Educational Centre. Food is also availed to the pupils. Thus far restoration Academy has had hundreds of graduates from the Academy.

Good Samaritan Counteracts Hydroplaning
by Morgan Crumm

I always get Fultondale and Gardendale confused. Though I've beaten down the stretch of I-65 between Nashville and Montgomery more times than I can count, it's been so long since I've passed through those Birmingham suburbs that I can't quite remember if it was the overpass at Mt. Olive Rd or Walker Chapel.

I remember it was raining.

My gold '95 4Runner was loaded down with most of what I owned, trucking me back to Auburn for another semester. Needing gas and coffee, I steered the Toyota toward the next exit and made a hard left turn onto the overpass.

I'd only hydroplaned once before--my car kissed a curb in minimal traffic on Maryland Way in Brentwood, TN going roughly 25 miles an hour. I was terrified for a third of a second, and then I was on my way and not a minute late for school.

This time would be different.

As I turned onto the overpass, I lost control of the vehicle. The car skidded ahead and made I don't know how many revolutions before the barrier wall broke its fall. If the car had been more top-heavy, or if my guardian angel had called in sick that day, I am confident I would have flipped off the over pass and reunited with I-65. When I found myself alive in a world that had finally stopped spinning, I felt stunned, speechless, terrified, and blessed.

My car would have to be towed—that was a given. I had an AAA card, but my cell phone had just died, and I couldn't find my charger. The nearest gas station was within sight, but a good hike down and past the treacherous and traffic-heavy overpass. . .in the cold, biting rain.

As I scanned the back of the car for any signs of my rain jacket, a blue Dodge Caravan pulled up next to me on the shoulder of the road. A petite woman got out and knocked on my window. "Do you need any help?" she asked.

"Come sit in the van and get out of the cold. It's messy, but it's warm." There were a toddler and an infant in car seats, and children's toys scattered throughout. She had noticed my Williamson County tags and my Auburn stickers and mentioned that she had family in Brentwood and had attended Auburn herself. Her husband was a minister at the nearby Baptist church. She let me use her cell phone and drove me down to the gas station so I could wait for the tow truck at the attached restaurant instead of in my cold, broken car.

Her kindness to me that day makes me tear up even now. I had never experienced an event as utterly terrifying as the wreck I had that day. And I had never experienced such unsolicited kindness from a stranger.

I pass people with broken down cars on the side of the road all the time. I'd love to tell you I make a point of stopping to help them. The truth is I don't, and I probably never will. I've heard too many stories and read too many "forward this to every female you know" chain-emails where that situation ends poorly for me to ever take the chance. But every time I see someone with car trouble, I think about the woman outside of Birmingham, the minister's wife from Gardendale or Fultondale. I think about how I can apply her Samaritan's spirit to the way I look at the world. Maybe I won't get out of my car for the person on the side of the road, but somewhere there is someone I can help right now. What am I doing to find that person?

EBONY

by Marjie Smith

I am ebony;

My brown parchment

stretched over my living carcass,

I sit and wait for death.

My folded bones fit together

like pieces of a wooden jigsaw.

I am the Africana statue you picked out

from where I sat beside the jade Buddha

in your city emporium.

The artist carved a lie:

He left off the flies and dust,

and hollowness of hunger.

I sit silent upon your shelf,

another forgotten treasure

displayed among your salvage

from past spending sprees.

Encased in dust,

I witness murder as I gaze down

at your laden table, your over-stuffed bellies

and your padded chairs.

You bought me and forsook me;

my hunger is your sales slip,

my squalor your income tax receipt,

and my draining life,

the nail that sealed your conscience shut.

History: While living in a small northern town in the mid-1980s, a group of women from a small Bible study group tried to raise money to assist World Vision with famine relief. We tried to encourage families to give up their family allowance benefits for one month. Unfortunately, it was primarily the women in the study who participated. It was a disappointing sum sent off to World Vision.

We sent the money to World Vision just before heading out of town for a few days. Distressed at the lack of response, I picked up an envelope that I had just opened after a stop at the post office. As my husband drove, I wrote the above poem on the back of the envelope, spilling out my frustration on paper.

The Winding Path Between the Trees
by Margaret Siegrist

The winding path between the trees
Those giants that perch to oversee
The hushed and languid morning sound
That dawn pulls gently from the ground
And with it fairy butterflies
Flitting their secret winged replies
Like sheets of rain the light descends
Pouring through the canopied den
A low wind blows up o'er the hill
It bids response with echoed trill
And swooping slowly to implore
An owl dips past the leafy floor
Scampering squirrels like hunted prey
Leave acorned treasures in dismay
As unpretentious deer turn round
And chipmunks ply beneath the ground
The winding path between the trees
Winding up past the quiet breeze
Like a tale that is never told
A sacred secret to unfold
An ancient tale, a forest song
That beckons those who hear its throng
And tread so lightly on the ground
Their silent echoes leave no sound

Have you ever felt like a leper?
by Marilyn Denney Blankenship

Have you ever felt like a leper?

I have.

When you felt like an outcast,
Who was there for you?
When you were in your mire, did anyone
avoid interfacing or connecting with you?
Did you feel alone and isolated in your suffering?
Were there even spiritual friends who dropped you?

In the midst of trials, or judgments, where you felt like a leper,
Were there true friends who actually moved toward you?
Did one, two, three or a handful of friends actually move into your pain
and walk beside you?

Such true friends are the salt of the earth.
These true friends are like the first crocus of spring.
These true friends are the sun backlighting clouds, peeking from behind
the clouds.
Faithful friends are fragrances of Christ, spreading the perfume of His
grace.

It doesn't take many true friends to help us endure suffering.
One or two encouraging faithful friends can help us survive
a crisis, a dark period of trial, or even recurring depression.

God has blessed me with such dear friends.
How blessed to have even one such friend, present in my life.
Thank you God for brave friends willing to enter dark places.

Thank you God for faithful friends who care and listen.
Such friends are like Jesus here in the flesh.
Such friends embody Christ for me.

I am so grateful for friends who represent the sweet aroma of Christ.

You do not have to be great, rich or powerful to have a few friends.

Practice being a friend, deepen relationships, and develop a few true friends.

These friends let you know you are not a leper. You are a precious child of God.

Francis Describes New Life Restoration Ministry

My name is Francis Njoroge. Formerly I was a street boy which I became after I nearly died because of hunger and starvation. Then I was a very little child and I also had a little brother by the name John Kamau whom we together joined the Springs of Life children's home but he later ran and went back to the street life. I went through a very difficult experience in the street which was a little bit better compared to the one that I had when I was living with my lovely late grandmother. This is because back in the street we could barely go without food since every trash was food unlike my late grandma's place where we could even go for a whole week without food. To me, joining Springs of Life children's home was a dream come true and also a prayer answered. On the other hand it was also miracle directly from God after He heard my cries. Without knowing the whereabouts of my relatives, mum Grace together with bishop Paul took me in and later they did some research and found out about my people and they spoke to my late grandma who was then both my father and mother. They informed her that I would be living in the home and this was an idea which she not only agreed with but also became very happy. Knowing that her grandchild was going to school was enough for her.

I was taken to school and what was so interesting is that I looked better compared to other kids who had two parents because when it came to the issues of text books, I and my other fellow kids from the Springs of Life Children's home had the required books plus the extras. Mum, Grace and Bishop made sure we were never sent home for any thing including fees.

I did my class eight in 2009 and qualified to join high school. Mum and Bishop Paul took me and my friend to one of the best provincial high schools of the time. Though the fees was very much, mum and Bishop Paul made sure that we reported with everything that was required and just like in primary, we were also better off compared to other students and in fact, most of my friends were shocked to know that I was once a street boy (Chokoraa) and that I was living in a children's home. There were times that we were sent home for school fees' balances. When we called our mum and told her about it she would not allow us to come home instead she would do her best and eventually sent the school fees through the phone and we would go back to class. They were very supporting until I did my exam in2013

I remember very well how mum Grace was troubled when we almost lost the chance of doing the K.C.S.E due to luck of the birth certificate, an important document before registering for national examination. Mum did all she could and we got the certificates and mine was processed while there and the next day I went and took the certificate to school and was registered for the exam.

Springs of Life has given me so much to count but to mention just but a few, I was given a home, a family, education, food, good health, clothing, the word of God and most importantly, love. For sure if they had given me everything and denied me love, I would have gone back to the street.

Though there were times I missed my mother and wished she was alive, love is the greatest and the most important gift mum grace and bishop Paul together with the family of Springs of Life has given me. Due to their love I have now become a better man with visions and dreams that I know trembles the devil.

I now have hope and a desire to live and make a good thing out of my life. At Springs of Life is where I realized the world had so much for me.

Springs of Life made me see the world and life in general in different perspective. Not everybody is mean and in fact mean people are very minimal because there are some people who cared for me.

I also realized that God had given the gift of writing and singing too. As if what mum and bishop Paul had given me was not enough they also supported my music and that really encouraged me. Nobody but God alone can pay mum and bishop for what they have done and given me.

Francis Njoroge is what is in my birth certificate but the name that I use most as a musician and I also love and prefer is **GITRAH** standing for **G**od **Is T**he **R**eason **A**m **H**ere.

Let the name of God he exalted Amen.

GOD BLESS SPRINGS OF LIFE CHILDREN'S RESTORATION CENTRE.

Motto: "ENABLED TO ENABLE OTHERS"

- GITRAH

Richard Visits Kibera
by Richard B. Anderson

12-Year-Old Girl: "Mom, how can the same God who created Maasi Mara allow such poverty in the Kibera slums?"

Mom: "Honey, I don't quite know how to answer that. . ."

We've all wondered. . .we've all asked similar questions. . .

This is the question: "How could a loving God allow evil/suffering in the world?"

I met the Mom in the airport in Nairobi. A large group of people had on the same-colored t-shirts. The message on their shirts said something to the effect of "Changing the World. . .One Life at a Time."

I asked her where they were from. She said that they were from Kansas City. They had come to Kenya to visit the young ladies in a girl's school which they sponsor. While there, they did some work—various odd jobs—at the school.

After ministering in Kibera, they wrapped up their mission trip with a safari to Maasi Mara. (I have come to understand that the word "safari" in Kenya simply means "vacation"—it does not necessarily mean an excursion to go and hunt big game.)

There is, evidently, a beautiful beach at Maasi Mara. The KC group took their R & R at the beach—processing what they had just seen, heard, touched, smelled, and tasted in Kibera. Hence her daughter's question.

Our friends Jay and Margaret were on our mission team—along with two of their children, Megan and Taylor. Before we left, a friend asked Jay (somewhat derisively), "What do you want to go to Africa for? With all that poverty, how much good can you do? You can't save 'em all."

Jay responded with a great analogy. "What if you were standing on an observation deck at Niagara Falls. All of a sudden a dam breaks

19

upstream. You see hundreds of people floating down the river—about to cascade over the falls. One is coming close enough to you for you to reach out and pull to safety. Would you not save the one—just because you can't save them all?" Brilliant!

This was the "crux" of our mission trip to Kenya. It was actually multi-faceted.

There were eighteen of us from the States. We were from various parts of the country.

We ministered in Nairobi the first half of the trip. We traveled by bus ten hours to a rural town called Malaba—on the Ugandan border—for the second half of our trip. One group taught SODIS—Solar Disinfecting—a water purification process/system.

One group taught them how to make biofuel briquettes out of leaves, paper, trash, etc. (They use charcoal to heat/cook with. This not only gets expensive, but depletes the tree/lumber supply in their area.)

Another group taught candle-making. Another soap-making. Another embroidery (they make unbelievable bags, purses, and other items out of plastic grocery bags.) In short, we were trying to teach them things which they could sell and generate some income.

My wife Cindy—along with Margaret, Megan, and Taylor—worked with little children, teaching them songs of worship. (THEY taught us how to worship. . .)

I got to preach in a church in Nairobi with a Swahili interpreter at my side. I got to speak in chapel at a Christian school in Kibera. . .just as Pastor Paul had spoken in our Christian school the prior spring.

The folks in Kenya have so little. . .but they have Jesus. . .and they worship Him. . .and their JOY is contagious!

Soli Deo Gloria. To God Alone be the Glory for His Body. . .

When Somebody Helped Me
by Rebecca Blankenship Papin

When I was 17, I came back from a 3-week trip to Europe. Completely broke when I arrived at JFK Airport, I did not even have a dollar to buy a Diet Coke. My debit card was overdrawn and I couldn't take any money out. I didn't think it mattered, though, since I had a connecting flight home to Nashville 3 hours later.

Unfortunately, I realized that my next flight was out of LaGuardia airport. The airport transfer cost $12. Calling my Dad, we tried to find a car service that would accept his credit card over the phone. No go.

Defeated, I walked up to the Information Desk and explained my story to a young woman before bursting into tears. She calmly reached into the cash register and handed me $16. "This is enough money for you to pay for your transfer and get a cup of coffee as well," she told me. I thanked her profusely, and, as my tears dried, walked away to pay for my airport transfer.

Seventeen years later, I still think that this was one of the nicest things that anyone ever did for me.

Barren Soldiers
by Margaret Siegrist

As barren soldiers line
  The field
The silent forest
  Heroes yield
Warriors to their death
  They stand
Under nature's
  Silent hand
Branches at their feet
  Betray
Former grandeur
  Now decay
Vigilantes
  Guarding fate
Posted at
  This woodland gate
Rising from
  The leafy floor
Proudly as
  If called to war
By some secret
  Battle horn
Triumphant on
  This misty morn.

Fall
by Margaret Siegrist

Twirling and whirling
The leaves in the trees
They're descending, unending
They fly as they please.

Raining and painting
The forest, a chorus
Uplifting, they're drifting
Out over the trees.

The beauty surrendered in autumn
How easy it seems to be
How odd that the maples surrender
Their blanket of vanity.

Chaotic, hypnotic
The leaves in the trees
They are turning and burning
The ground at our knees.

They're dripping then dipping
They're falling then stalling
They're flying then dying
With unaltered ease.

The leaves in the trees
They're falling and falling and falling
They're falling and calling and falling
Falling and falling.

Ministry is about determination
by Rev. Raphael Nzau

Ministry is a calling. The Almighty God deals with the heart of a man He wants to use to a point of answering to the call. It has to be with a sure confirmation that God has called one to a specific ministry. This assurance indeed helps in times of trials that rock against one's ministry unexpectedly. The assurance and confirmation of call will keep a minister going regardless of the roughness and toughness of the road to destiny.

As an associate minister to Bishop Paul Mbithi of New Life Restoration Ministries International, since 1997, I, Rev. Raphael Nzau have always embarked on a pursuit for destiny for myself and many others in the ministry. The Lord has been faithful and has not allowed that we suffer beyond what we can be able to bear. Being located in the heart of East and Central Africa's largest and the poorest slum, as ministry headquarters, we have been through numerous challenges. This is Kibera slums in Nairobi, Kenya. These include crime escalation, financial and psychosocial problems that require God's intervention.

It has not been easy to preach the gospel to a people with an empty stomach, when in reality they were used to earning their livelihood through crime related means like prostitution, stealing, drug abuse and robbery. As a result men and women have suffered HIV and AIDS infectious diseases, leading to death and subsequently leaving behind many orphans that are hopeless. God in His faithfulness has helped New Life Restoration Ministries International to establish an orphanage (children's home) and a kindergarten and primary school, that up to date has not been capable to at least pay the teachers and workers since a good number of the children are from the orphanage.

However, we join Dr. Robert Schuller in the thought of the title of his book "Tough Times Never Last, But Tough People Do". Our ministry has been through tough moments. The Bishop Plays the tough one's position and I follow him as he follows Christ in the game. The ministry name, New Life RESTORATION Ministries, carries the full theme and core value of the ministry. We are called in ministry to Restore: -

- ➤ Sinners to Christ
- ➤ The hopeless to the hope of God
- ➤ The lost back to the way
- ➤ The poor to riches in Christ
- ➤ Orphans to live like with Parents
- ➤ Courage to those with broken hearts

All the above can be done through preaching of the Gospel of hope, except providing parenthood to the orphaned. This one must apply practically to life. Their empty bellies need food, homelessness needs housing and all amenities that go by it. They need more than a gospel of words but rather of deeds.

We have covered some distance and still have along way to go. The destiny is now clearer than when we first began, 17 years ago. We hope in the Lord to cover the remaining course.

God bless the reader

Rev. Raphael Nzau – email-rmnzau@yahoo.com

My Father's Love
by Kathy Edwards

My father was a thinker, an artist and a lover of beauty. He loved making things and especially loved to make them with my brother and me.

One March, 57 years ago when I was 9 years old, he designed the most intricate, beautiful box-kite I could imagine and let me put on the finishing touches. An especially windy day, I enthusiastically toted the lightweight but large flyer out of my front door and had not even gone half a block with it when an unexpected whoosh of wind released the kite from my little fingers.

Close to tears, I ran after it but could not catch it. I sorrowfully walked back home wondering how I could ever have let something so wonderful as the box kite my daddy designed and made for me escape my hand.

Feeling like a terrible disappointment to my father and expecting punishment for my incompetence, I tearfully told him my sad saga.

He explained that the value of the box kite was in our time together and the love we shared and there was nothing to feel badly about.

Never have I felt so validated and loved. He had just given me the best gift that he could ever give me: he paved the way for me to understand the unconditional love of my heavenly Father.

Lake Fog
by Margaret Siegrist

The slow and silent fog
Folds itself around the waters edge
And spreads its misty blanket
O'er the mirrored bed.
I shudder,
For I should know this place, this lake.
And yet she hides
Till light betrays her faceless form
And lifts this misty veil.

The Power of Words to Turn People Around
by Read Blankenship

A teen I had known since early adolescence began using drugs. His personality went from open and inviting to distant and reserved.

After a couple of years of using, I confronted him.

I told him what initially drew me to him: ambition, faith, and standing up to be the only drug-free person in his group- basically things most teens don't have. These things are gone now but are not too late to get back, I told him. He heard me out but clearly was not interested in any input I had regarding his drug use.

About five years later, I got a message from him on Facebook. He now works in film production and is very active in his church. The purpose of his message to me was gratitude- gratitude for a conversation that turned his life around.

I am His Delight
by Margaret Siegrist

I came in fear and barrenness
to where my Savoir stood
He placed on me a robe of red
and gently raised its hood.

And watching as he tied the cloak
His righteousness imbued
I felt an overwhelming sense
My joy had been renewed.

God alone is my salvation
Defender from all shame
He also clothes me with his honor
Calling me by name.

A deep and welling overarching
Haven in the night
The peace I feel is from a knowing
I am his delight.

A word from John Ouya, one of the orphanage's residents

The Springs of Life children's restoration center is a place of giving back. Thanks to the guys like me so far so good we give God all the glory for all that happened and also what is in the future to come because I really know it is greater than what has happened.

And as I know there is a reason why the Springs of Life home was set up at the market. God did not do a mistake neither had he mistakenly given mum Grace and bishop Paul Mbithi a vision and ambitions to start the orphanage. Thanks and all appreciation be to God and no one else.

I as John Ouya, I came to the orphanage when I was young without knowing the four cardinal points of the compass. What do I mean? My life had no direction, messed up, dirty indeed, confused, someone who was not reliable and did not have a goal in life. This is because there was no one and nothing to motivate me and show me the right direction in the compass.

East or west I always found restoration center is the best home I found for many young living on the street   boys and girls who don't have hope in life .at the orphanage we have never lacked food, shelter and clothing. Thanks to mum grace - bravo - through the help of God, our living has been so smooth. But also there have been so many challenges, the break out of fire. All in all mum and bishop have been so close to us and encourage us how to move on and cope with life no matter whether you found yourself between a rock and a hard surface. God is always there for us all.

We have been brought up in a Christian environment, which is the better option. Education has given us general knowledge, life skills and other knowledge, which is also a basic need. As God continues to use mum and bishop, may He also remember their needs and sustain them in their daily life

God bless.

My Aunts
by Margaret Siegrist

I can still see my two sweet aunts sitting right there at the kitchen table.
Right there in their bathrobes with their coffee and their " I declares"
and their toast and laughing and smoking and sipping. Mostly laughing
....and lots of "Lord have mercies", and talking about cousins and
smoking some more.

They had curlers and chenille robes and house shoes and built fires in
the mornings. It was almost a sacred kind of time, those mornings. I
never wanted them to end.   Aunt Betty was really short but she always
seemed like a big kind of person to me. Aunt Jane was really tall but
never intimidating and as they sat across from each other, they had a
kind of knowing, a kind of likeness to each other. Both were kind and
funny and when they got together, the laughter seemed contagious.

As I sat with my cereal bowl, I would study their smoking and listen to
their stories, which always seemed interesting because they were
always about people. Their kitchens were safe kind of places. I felt I
could tell them anything but mostly I just liked listening. Both of my
aunts are gone now but I can still see, smell and hear that kitchen and
most of all feel the joy around that table. It really wasn't about the
conversation, or the coffee or the smoking (well maybe the smoking) or
the cereal. It was really about feeling a sense of belonging.

I miss them both.

Juliana speaks of Kibera

My name is Juliana Mutheu Nchebere. Paul and Grace Mbithi are my amazing parents. They started New Life Restoration Ministries when I was just 11 years old almost turning 12. We had been going to one of the mainstream churches for about a year and one day dad says we get ready for church. So we assume we would be going to our normal church then we ask why are we setting up the house yet we are about to leave and he says that we are having church at home. And that was our first service - it was Mum, Dad, Ben, myself and two of my cousins with our house assistant at that time. That was quite an experience having church at home. But the most amazing thing, we grew in our house. People started inviting other people and we became bigger than our house and had to move to a bigger space. The one thing I loved was the feeling of family that we had, we all knew each other and their children and loved and fellowshipped together. We used to have juice and biscuits after service which is something that I do miss because it made sure people got to talk and know each other better and maintain the unity of family.

As the church grew so did we and we became even more aware of the calling of God on our parents' lives. The one thing I celebrate the most is my parents' love and willingness to make a difference in the lives of the people in Kibera. They had the option of setting up church in the more affluent areas but they have stuck to their calling and continued to minister to the people in the less affluent neighborhoods and changed the lives of the people there. Even if it's with the smallest things as having a family Sunday where we ate meals together. The children's home and the passion that mum and dad have to ensure that the children get food, shelter, clothing, education, emotional support and a proper upbringing is amazing. That they both left their jobs to serve and make a difference is something that only God would be able to reward them.

It has not been an easy journey for us as the children. We may have missed the joys of being in a proper teens Sunday school class and having church friends that are of the same age and share the same views or have things in common with, but what made it easier was knowing that they are doing their level best to bring us up in a way that honors God and also making a difference in the society. Another good that came from it was I learnt that I can make a good Sunday school teacher, I used to teach the younger children, that was so much fun but tiring. It was a little hard not having all the things other people in school had because money may have been a little tight and the children in the home needed food and other things. They really did an amazing job with us and I am super grateful and proud of them.

That is my story; I have amazing parents who do such amazing things to 'the least of these'. I normally say if I turn out to be half of the people that they are I would have lived and been an amazing person.

God Bless and if you can do anything to support the work they do here in Kenya, please do.

Best Regards,

Juliana Nchebere.

Classroom Help for a New Teacher-to-be
by Heather Barr

The stress and anxiety of my first field placement had been eating away at my mind for weeks. Becoming a teacher was far more troubling than I had ever imagined. After being in a classroom last semester with a teacher who hardly acknowledged my existence, I had minuscule hopes for my new placement.

On my first day, I was unable to eat breakfast because my stomach was too full of nerves. I just knew I would not be received warmly by my new teacher.

When I finally arrived at the school, I was met with the warmest, biggest smile I had ever seen. My new mentor introduced me to the 24 second graders as if I was the biggest celebrity that ever lived. She then presented me a gift on behalf of herself and the students.

She assured me the students would love me and that I would be a huge hit in the classroom. I have never felt so welcomed, or accepted, by a complete stranger in my life.

Because of her thoughtfulness and compassion, I was on top of the world and totally at ease. I hope one day I can be that guiding teacher for a new, scared, eager teacher-to-be.

The very Heart of Jesus
by Gail Castle

Scripture Reading: Matthew 25:31 – 46

On the road, traveling from place to place, meeting and interacting with people is where we come face to face with Jesus's love and message and our participation in and response to His love and message. It is this face-to-face interaction that we can begin to live out the calling and mandate of our faith as Christians. I often question the existence of the institution of Church because of the country club mentality that can settle into its very being and purpose of existence.

We can so easily get sidetracked from the real mission of being a disciple of and in relationship with Jesus because of our country club and social club mentalities…. How big and pretty are our church buildings, programs, budgets, staff positions etc… We become paralyzed in our faith because we get comfortable and complacent in our plush pews and insulate ourselves from the people of our world who are in need with the houses we live in and the cars we drive. It is easy to stay in our comfortable places.

Jesus teaches his audience (me and you) through parables to make a point, to catch us off guard because we live so much of our lives not being able to see the forest for the trees. He wants us to get outside of our comfortable places and mentalities. He wants us to move and do….it is all about action… giving and receiving His love because that is what has lasting power.

Jesus was all about action and getting us to move out of our own understanding of life. His commandments require us to move and do, give and receive. Matthew 25:31 – 46 is a wonderful parable teaching us that the very relationship and meaning of life in and with Jesus is about giving to and doing for those in need.

When you go and do and get out of the pew and move from place to place and interact face to face, the very heart of Jesus becomes your heart and his message and love is then transferred to another, one to another.

Helping, volunteering, giving of yourself and resources is touching the robe and the very heart of Jesus. We can only find true fulfillment and healing when we give ourselves one to another, to help someone in need, volunteer, go and feed, cloth, attend to, build, teach, share, pray with, etc... and see how your life and the other life is transformed by the power of this action. "The King will answer and say to them, 'Truly I say to you, to the extent that you did it to one of these brothers of mine, even the least of them, you did it to Me.' Matthew 25:40

Devotional Prayer: Dear gracious and loving Father, thank you for your son who gave the ultimate gift of love (himself) by dying on the cross to save us from our sins so that we may have eternal life with you. I pray for the courage to go, to do, and to give of myself to someone in need.

Dedication: To Bishop Paul and Grace Mbithi and all of the sisters and brothers at New Life Restoration Ministries in Nairobi Kenya in the Kibera (slums). Thank you for being examples of people living out the very heart of Jesus.

CS Lewis on Helping

Nothing that you have not given away will ever be really yours.
— CS Lewis

The task of the modern educator is not to cut down jungles, but to irrigate deserts.
— CS Lewis

Miracles are a retelling in small letters of the very same story which is written across the whole world in letters too large for some of us to see.
— CS Lewis

Friends
by Anonymous

Friends.
Give me more than a hug.
Give me more than a compliment about my t-shirt.
Tell me if I have done something that meant something to them.
Tell me if I have done something to hurt them.
Forgive me.
Caution me.
Give me more then a round of their favorite game.
Hold me accountable.

Friends.
Let me also hold you accountable.
Let me give you more than a hug.
Permit me to encourage you to use your gifts.
Permit me to tell you if something you did hurt me.
Let me forgive you, too.
Please, let me give you my caution when I am concerned.
All because I DO love you.
Please, let me help keep you accountable, too.

Oh Holy Father

by Margaret Siegrist

We bow before you
And ask that we might see your face
Draw us inward
Through the curtain
To your mercy seat of grace
Grace so deep and long and wide
Grace that sin cannot deny
Grace for us
Grace for us

Unfailing grace for us
Oh Faithful Spirit
We come before you
And ask that you would rend our hearts
Draw the veil from every vision
So that we may know in part
Know how deep and long and wide
Is the love the crucified
Has for us
Has for us

What New Life Restoration Ministry has meant to Catherine

My name is Catherine.

I got married to my husband, Raphael, while he was serving in a certain church in the early (1990) nineties and we both loved the Lord Jesus and attended church faithfully.

A time came when I personally felt that I am not really getting enough spiritual nourishment in this church and I mentioned this to my husband who was the head usher by then and he could hear none of this.

As time went by, I started defying my husband's orders to attend this church and started going to a different one, thus putting my family unity and peace in jeopardy.

This angered my husband and even brought a great rift in our relationship.

He insisted that we should not be going to different churches as a couple but I continued disobeying him and I was ready for anything else but not back to that church.

It is during this period that New Life Restoration Ministries came into existence.

We both agreed to leave our respective places of worship and join the ministry, a move that brought reconciliation and healing to my young family.

I am forever grateful to God for this ministry and I normally refer to it as a rescuer of my family and marriage.

Today, we are pastoring a branch church of New Life Restoration Ministries at a place called Mlolongo which is one and a half years old after being assistants at the ministry headquarters in Kibera for more than fifteen years under Bishop Paul and pastor Grace Mbithi. God came in our family through New Life Restoration Ministries and rescued my family as the Bible says two cannot walk together unless they agree.

To God be the glory. Amen

Catherine

His deathless love for us
by Margaret Siegrist

Oh Lamb of Heaven

We fall before you

As we gather round your throne

All the angels

Hushed in silence

As your mercy calls us home

Mercy deep and long and wide

Mercy calling to its bride

Calling us

Calling us

Your mercy calls to us

Your mercy calls to us

The Pontiac and the Mercedes

A man was driving his car, when he saw an old lady, stranded on the side of the road. He saw that she needed help. So he stopped his Pontiac near her Mercedes and got out.

He smiled, while he was approaching her, still she was worried, as nobody had stopped for hours. Moreover, he did not look safe, as his appearance was so poor and shabby. He could see, how frightened she was, so he tried to calm her: „ I'm here to help you, don't worry. My name is Bryan Anderson".

The tire was flat, so he had to crawl under the car. While changing the tire, he got dirty and his hands were hurt.

When the job was done, she asked how much she owed him for his help. Bryan smiled. He said: 'If you really want to pay me back, the next time you see someone, who needs help, give that person the needed assistance. And think of me'.

Later the same evening, the lady stopped by a small cafe. That place looked dingy. Then she saw a waitress, nearly eight months pregnant, wiping her wet hair with a towel. The waitress had a sweet friendly smile, although she had spent on her feet the whole day.

The lady wondered, how someone, who has so little, could be so kind and giving to a stranger. Then she remembered Bryan.

The lady had finished her meal and paid with a hundred dollar bill. The waitress went to get change and when she came back, the lady was gone. She left a note on the napkin: 'you don't own me anything. Somebody once helped me, just like now I'm helping you. If you really want to pay me back, do not let this chain of love end with you'. The waitress found four more one hundred bills under the napkin.

43

That night the waitress came home earlier. She was thinking about the lady and the money she left. She was wondering, how the lady could know how much she and her husband needed it. Especially now, when the baby will soon arrive. She knew, that her husband worried about that, so she was glad to tell him good news.

Then she kissed him and whispered, "Now everything will be all right. I love you, Bryan Anderson".

- Popular motivational story about giving

Welcome to Your Ride
by Trevor Johnston

Welcome to your motorcycle.

Don't be afraid.

What you are feeling is the wind on your skin.

You cannot see it, but you can feel it and sense its presence.

Around you are your family members.

Some of them are older and some of them are younger.

The various motorcycles and their sounds can't help but draw attention.

You seem to be having fun. "Weird," some people think "...they seem to be enjoying themselves...hmm."

You are not worried about what you have on, and you have on a helmet.

Some people want to tell you to take it off. You keep it on, believe you need protection.

You remind yourself not to look back. You need to keep your eyes on the road.

You feel the beauty all around you when things are beautiful. A storm comes and you take refuge with your family under an acceptable overpass. You tell jokes, share stories. Some of your friends and you feel a little sore. Perhaps the storm can work for good. Rest.

The storm passes and you are back on the ride and you are feeling wind and finding fun.

Welcome to life with Jesus Christ.

Do not be afraid.

What you are feeling is the beginning of a relationship.

You cannot see it, but others can see it when you live your lifestyle of Christ-love.

You are around God's family. People of each race, gender, and generation are with you.

The diversity of life, all unified, is attracting some attention.

You are worshipping the Living God, Immanuel, together. You are too busy experiencing life and peace to care what others think about you.

You wear salvation like a helmet. Satan told you that you would look cooler without it. You chose God's truth about who you are, rather than worldly opinions about what is cool.

You don't return to your childish ways because you have matured to seek the Prize promised to you by Faith.

God is showing you that he makes everything beautiful in His time. In the mean time, He is blessing you with faithfulness in His Kingdom, no matter where He leads you.

Trials do not last forever. You are riding on to heaven, to eternal life with Jesus Christ.

Small Child Learns about Giving
by Morgan Crumm

"Mommy, what is serving?" a small child asked one day.
"It's helping other people, like sharing when you play,"
Mom smiled and thought a little more about what she should say.

"Bringing food to those who hunger and blankets to the cold,
Finding homes for orphaned babies and assistance for the old." "
But how can I serve God?" the child demanded to be told.

The mother's heart was touched, and she responded on a whim,
"Always think of others and what you can give to them.
When you give to other people, you also give to Him."

Disappointment 101
by Terry Blankenship

There was a job that I really, really wanted.

And I thought I got it. I was even notified that I got it. I was ecstatic. I thanked God over and over.

But I was notified about 5 hours later that the offer was rescinded. I was crushed. I was angry at God. I was confused. Then I turned the anger on myself. I was a loser, I told myself. I was a joke. I was no good.

Isn't this the journey that disappointment takes in us? This is true for me and I suspect that this may be true for you also.

Think about a disappointment you have had. Now let's get our arms around it.

As a Christian, we must put this in God's hands. I mean, we have to ... there is really no other option.

God promises that 'all things work together for the good for those who love God and are called according to his purpose.'

In my case, I had to believe that it was God's will that the door to the job was slammed shut. Perhaps I would have suffered something that was not good in the new job and God spared me from it. Perhaps there was an opportunity that was better for me that I would not have been available for. Who knows?

Our Father does.

What about your disappointment?

Have you given your disappointment to God yet? Or are you still in the spin cycle of disappointment, going round and round?

Let me challenge you to give your disappointment to God. You will not have peace in your heart until you do.

How do you turn your disappointment over to God?

You pray. You communicate with God. You say, 'God, I turn this disappointment over to you. I give you all of the circumstances, all of my hurt and confusion. I trust you with this disappointment and ask you to help me move through this. Help me gain wisdom from this disappointment. Amen'

It is crucial that you seek wisdom from any and all disappointments that you endure. Let's face it; disappointments are part of the stuff of which life is made.

Some people allow disappointments to change the course of their lives. For the worse. You do not want this to be you. You do not want to be the one who encounters a disappointment so large and so persistent that it knocks your life off course.

So let's review ... when faced with disappointment:

1. Nothing wrong with feeling bad about it for a short period of time ... that is part of being congruent with your feelings and being congruent. So don't beat yourself up over feeling down and confused when a disappointment comes your way - no matter the size.

2. Turn the disappointment over to God

3. Ask God for the wisdom that you need to glean from the disappointment.

By the way, that job disappointment I spoke of earlier?

The company went out of business about 6 months later.

Learning to handle disappointment as a stepping-stone rather than a millstone around your neck can be a key to growing in Christ.

Even More Wise Sayings about Helping

"When we give cheerfully and accept gratefully, everyone is blessed."
— Maya Angelou

"A kind gesture can reach a wound that only compassion can heal."
— Steve Maraboli, *Life, the Truth, and Being Free*

"You have not lived today until you have done something for someone who can never repay you."
— John Bunyan

"Doing nothing for others is the undoing of ourselves."
— Horace Mann

"No one is useless in this world who lightens the burdens of another."
— Charles Dickens

"There is no exercise better for the heart than reaching down and lifting people up."
— John Holmes

"No one has ever become poor by giving."
— Anne Frank

Winter
by Margaret Siegrist

Silently, on tiptoe, winter steals across the lake.
She wields and throws her icy cloak o'er unsuspecting prey
As pale and barren trees lift up their black and leafless limbs
They grasp and grope, they clap and sway, in unisoned applause.
And all things living hold their breath, a captive of this frigid play
Yet underneath the whiteness lies an echo deep and low
An ancient rhythmic lullaby that calls to all who hear
To all who listen, all who see beyond this snowy gauze.

Poem June 29, 2012
by Terry Blankenship

I love God more
 Than words can express
He touches my life
 I am always so blest

When his hand gently guides me
 I see his great love
It's then that I'm glad
 I am loved from above

Grudges don't stop me
 I throw them away
Envy can't harm me
 They don't get in my way

An avalanche of love
 Fell on me today
His mercy and his grace
 Illuminate my way

The Basketball and the Clarinet
by Terry Blankenship

Imagine being Michael Jordan - incredible at basketball - yet feeling like you needed to excel at being a clarinet player. You might go through life shooting a few hoops but you would train, train, train during your clarinet lessons, hoping to be the very best you could be, in order to live up to the expectations of others.

Meanwhile, your natural gift would languish, harpooned by those very expectations.

Carl Rogers is a writer whose writings I love.

By the way, he is the father of modern American psychology (and studied to be a Lutheran minister at one time).

He posits an interesting question for his readers: what is the meaning of life?

As Christians we understand the answer to be obvious but listen to how he answers the question, what is the meaning of life?

"To be that self which one truly is."

I'm sorry but that knocks my socks off and sets my hair on fire simultaneously.

I think it is truth that we Christians need sorely to hear ... no, not just hear but hear and digest.

He goes on to say that 'one is never more strong than when one is fully one's self'.

I think this has powerful ramifications for those wanting an authentic walk in Christ ... not an experience that has a shelf-life of just a few years. If you achieve authenticity in your life in Christ, you can fully expect to navigate life's mountains and valleys well (notice I said navigate, not avoid) and reach life's end stronger than you started.

You just have to relax into God's natural gifting for your life.

If you are a writer, write.

If you are a musician, play.

If you are a businessperson, deal.

If you are a chef, cook.

If you are a speechwriter, write speeches.

A city set on a hill cannot be hidden. When you embrace who you are in Christ, your light will never show more brightly. Your organic attributes that God put in your DNA will blaze forth, sending his fragrance everywhere.

In other words, being yourself is godly.

We all need to put down the clarinet and start playing basketball again.

Snowflakes

by Margaret Siegrist

Intrusive, elusive
They fly through the night
Frozen white comets
Flinging their light
Plunging to earth
An extinguishing flame
Melting the fire
They tenaciously claim.
Their light with each flicker
Betrays their last breath
Beauty transcendent
Even in death

Love Me

by Anonymous

Love me.
Don't love me because I deserve it.
Don't love me because I am easy to love.
Don't love me if I can repay you.
Love me because I need love, too.

Love me.
Don't love me because I make sense.
Don't love me because I am wise.
Love me even if I am different.
Love me even if I seem foolish.

That is the Love I need.
Do you clearly see my heart?
Jesus says I am wonderfully made.
Will you treat me like His art?
Love me.

Warren Buffett, Cicero and Booker T Washington
Speak about Helping

"Non nobis solum nati sumus. (Not for ourselves alone are we born.)"
— Cicero

"Those who are happiest are those who do the most for others."
— Booker T. Washington, *Up from Slavery*

"If you're in the luckiest one per cent of humanity, you owe it to the rest of humanity to think about the other 99 per cent."
— Warren Buffett

The Portal
by Margaret Siegrist

A vine loops round the willing tree

Its double arches form a V

And frame the secret portal door

That spreads across the forest floor.

Intrigued I peer within its realm

Where robins stand to guard the helm

And past the feathered watch I spy

Two deer in tranquil worship lie

As lacewings in their grand attire

Dart and flit as if on fire

And bunnies hopping ,hop, refrain

Dancing to disjointed strain.

I find myself suspended there

Enchanted by this ancient lair.

Who'd suspect a gate when flung

Such unexpected beauty hung.

The Old Tree

by Margaret Siegrist

The old tree hears the quiet wind
It sings beyond the silent lake
She nods and dips her withered hand
Across the glass and back again

Her barren face is turned and still
To catch springs long awaited breath
Betraying now her winter vows
As water echoes trace her boughs

And held in nature's mystic trance
Captive to some former glory
She knows that deep and distant pleas
Are answered in the voiceless breeze.

Sunset
by Terry Blankenship

The most life-giving people that I am ever around are those who are full of grace.

The most energizing people that I am ever around are those who accept me just like I am. And have given up trying to change me.

Have you ever been around someone who keeps trying to conform you into their own image of how you should be? It is uncomfortable and is much like using a key in a lock where the key is off just a little bit. Great effort might be expended in trying to get the lock unlocked but trust me, the key will break first.

Displaying grace and acceptance to others allows the key to unlock the lock every time.

Carl Rogers, the father of modern American psychology, said that one of the most difficult tasks for people is to accept others like they accept sunsets. When we step outside at night to view a sunset, we never say turn the pinks up and turn the blues down and then the sunset will be just right. No, we accept the beauty in the sunset just like it is.

Something tells me that when we accept others like we accept sunsets, we are displaying the grace of Christ to them. And grace is always, always, always transformational.

I am not good at this... As a matter of fact, I am pretty poor at it. But accepting others like I accept sunsets is how I want to be.

Homework: the next person that you meet, accept them exactly like you accept the sunset. Just the way they are. And let God do the work.

Anything else is exhausting and really doesn't produce much at all.

To the sunset!

Buzzards, tin cans and putting your car in reverse
by Terry Blankenship

When I was younger, my father would take my brother and me into the forest with our guns (we were old enough to have been taught gun safety) to target practice. It was called plinking. We would spend Sunday afternoons just plinking.

Our targets were as elusive as tin cans and coke bottles. We would also lie on our backs and shoot at buzzards as they circled high, high above us, looking for their next tasty meal.

The tin cans and cokes we often hit ... we never hit a buzzard.

But it didn't matter. We were with our father and having a great time.

After a while, we would pack up and head home.

Completely satisfied.

My father has been deceased over 20 years. Yet the memory of time spent with him is still satisfying, like a cool, refreshing breeze settling over my spirit.

Our heavenly father cannot be seen, touched or perceived by any of our 5 senses. Yet he is as real as my earthly father ever was.

The cool breeze inwardly that I feel when I think of my dad and those times with him is available to us with our heavenly father. The only difference as I see it is that there are no memories involved, it is a continuing present-day reality.

Persistent, viable and actual.

The outward world is often chaotic, rife with literal and figurative tornados, tsunamis and earthquakes.

Yet our inner world can be one of a protected harbor, a placid pond, a place of cool breezes.

Step back today from the rim of your personal volcano ... put your emotional car into reverse for just a moment today and back away from the grinding traffic jam that might be bottling your life ... close your eyes and spend time with your heavenly father.

The times of refreshing will surely be summoned to your spirit.

The Cold Wind
by Margaret Siegrist

Deep in recesses
  Where the dark shadows stir
And words lay dormant
  And dry
A cold wind blows
  Over souls who have died
And they shiver as the chill
  Passes by
No hope no hope apart from the Light

The Feast of the First Mowing
The Suburban Awakening of the Primal Man
by Gerrit Gustafson

(In the spring of 2011, David and Deen Logan, together with Gerrit and Himmie Gustafson re-instituted the long-neglected Feast of the First Mowing *in their Brenthaven neighborhood, Brentwood, TN. Here's the story behind that historic celebration...)*

Every spring, there is a week when lawnmowers all over suburban America are startled out of their groggy hibernation by the stumbling, but grizzled determination of their owners.

Somewhere deep in the masculine psyche, an urging has been awakened among these misplaced men of the woods, in much the same way as the voice of the full moon awakens the wolves' howling. The sound of lawnmower engines rise from one lawn, then ten, and then a hundred. The multiplied sounds become a vernal paean to the God of the Grass, saturating the heavens and bringing favor on all the land.

What has awakened this urging among these misplaced men of the woods? Now there's a great mystery! Some older men, who lived before the mowers, heard it said by their grandfathers, who heard it from the Indians, that the greening of the spring grass coincided with a deep sonic rumble that comes from the belly of the earth for several weeks near the end of winter, and the beginning of spring.

It is that deep sound that awakens the bears from their hibernation. And though man cannot *hear* the sound, he can *feel* it. This feeling triggered a script which had been woven into the core of his being from the dawn of creation. From the ancient writings, we learn that it was this sound that made the kings want to go out to war in the spring. It was this same sound that made the cowboys, who had been idled by the winter, want to saddle up again to go find new adventure.

This sub-sonic sense, however, is only known to the men; the women feel it not. They can only know it by the spark they see in the eyes of their men. "The old bears are awakening from their stupor," they would say with a smile, as they are sent to the station to fetch the gas. They are always glad when they see the men folk go out with a warrior's visage, saddle up on their lawnmowers like cowboys, and begin again to be revived from their muted manhood. The winter months are always a test, for then, the men seemed agitated, restless, bewildered and lost. Life is always difficult in the winter for the women.

But when the sounds of the mowers are first heard in the neighborhoods, the women begin to shout across the fences to one another, and to call to each other on the phones. Their men are happy again. And that makes the women happy too. So, years ago, they decided to have a feast. Thus the origin of *The Feast of the First Mowing*.

More than just the men getting out to cut the grass, the sound of the mowers is truly *The Suburban Awakening of the Primal Man,* or as the women sing in preparation for the feast *"The Old Bears are Awakening from Their Stupor!"*

So now, let all who gather, lift their glasses: *"Here's to a Joyous Feast of the First Mowing!!"*

Benediction
by Margaret Siegrist

May the love of Christ abide
And may his mercies never cease
May you ever be surrounded by
The presence of His peace.
May you hear the voice that calls
Deep and low in silence still
You are the one, I long have loved
Then and now, I love you still.

THE KIBERA WRITERS
(In alphabetical order)

Richard Anderson
Marilyn Denney Blankenship
Read Blankenship
Terry Blankenship
Gail Castle
Morgan Crumm
Catherine
Kathy Edwards
Gitrah
Gerrit Gustafson
Trevor Johnston
Juliana Mutheu Nchebere
Rev. Raphael Nzau
John Ouya
Rebecca Blankenship Papin
Margaret Siegrist
Marjie Smith

How to Pay for this Book Through St Bartholomew's Website

1) Take this book and promise to pay

2) Now, when you get home, go to www.stbs.net

3) You will pay through this website - it is important that in the category you choose 'New Life Restoration Ministry - Kenya'- and in the note field, write 'Book'

4) When you go to the website, you click GIVE

5) Next you come to the page where you designate what you are paying for. Enter $10.00 in the amount and that in the category you choose 'New Life Restoration Ministry - Kenya'- and in the note field, write 'Book'

6) You will have to sign up once and only once through Monk ID in order to do this. If you do not have a Monk ID, you will need to get one and it is super easy. That is where you enter your credit card info.

How to Pay for this Book by Mailing a Check

If you prefer, you can always mail a check made out to **'St Bartholomew's Episcopal Church'** for $10.00 with **'New Life Restoration Ministries Book' in the memo field** of the check. Mail the check to:

St Bartholomews
4800 Belmont Park Terrace
Nashville, TN 37215

REMEMBER YOU CAN SUPPORT THIS MINISTRY ON AN ONGOING BASIS BY GIVING REGULARLY THROUGH ST SB'S WEBSITE OR MAILING A CHECK!

THANK YOU!!